To Roger, fellow writer, with my best wishes!
Mary Mulhern

brides in black
mary ann mulhern

Black Moss Press
2012

Copyright © 2012 Mary Ann Mulhern

Library and Archives Canada Cataloguing in Publication
Mulhern, Mary Ann
  Brides in black / Mary Ann Mulhern.
Poems.
ISBN 978-0-88753-498-0

1. Nuns--Poetry. 2. Convents--Poetry. I. Title.

PS8576.U415B75 2012   C811'.6   C2012-901338-2

Interior Design: Celia Girgenti, Beth Harrett, Amelia Roy-Weber, Jaclyn Wood
Interior Art: Jacob Hickson
Cover Design: Sarah Benoit, Emily Buta, Ashley Gibb
Cover Art: Helen Girgenti
Palm Poets Series is designed by Karen Veryle Monck

Black Moss
EST. 1969 Press

Published by Black Moss Press at 2450 Byng Road, Windsor, Ontario, N8W 3E8 Canada. Black Moss books are distributed in Canada and the U.S. by LitDistCo. All orders should be directed to LitDistCo. Black Moss Press books can also be found on our website www.blackmosspress.com. Black Moss would like to acknowledge the generous financial support from both the Canada Council for the Arts and the Ontario Arts Council.

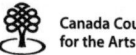 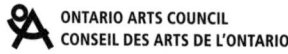

PRINTED IN CANADA

Names and identifying details of some individuals have been changed to protect their privacy.

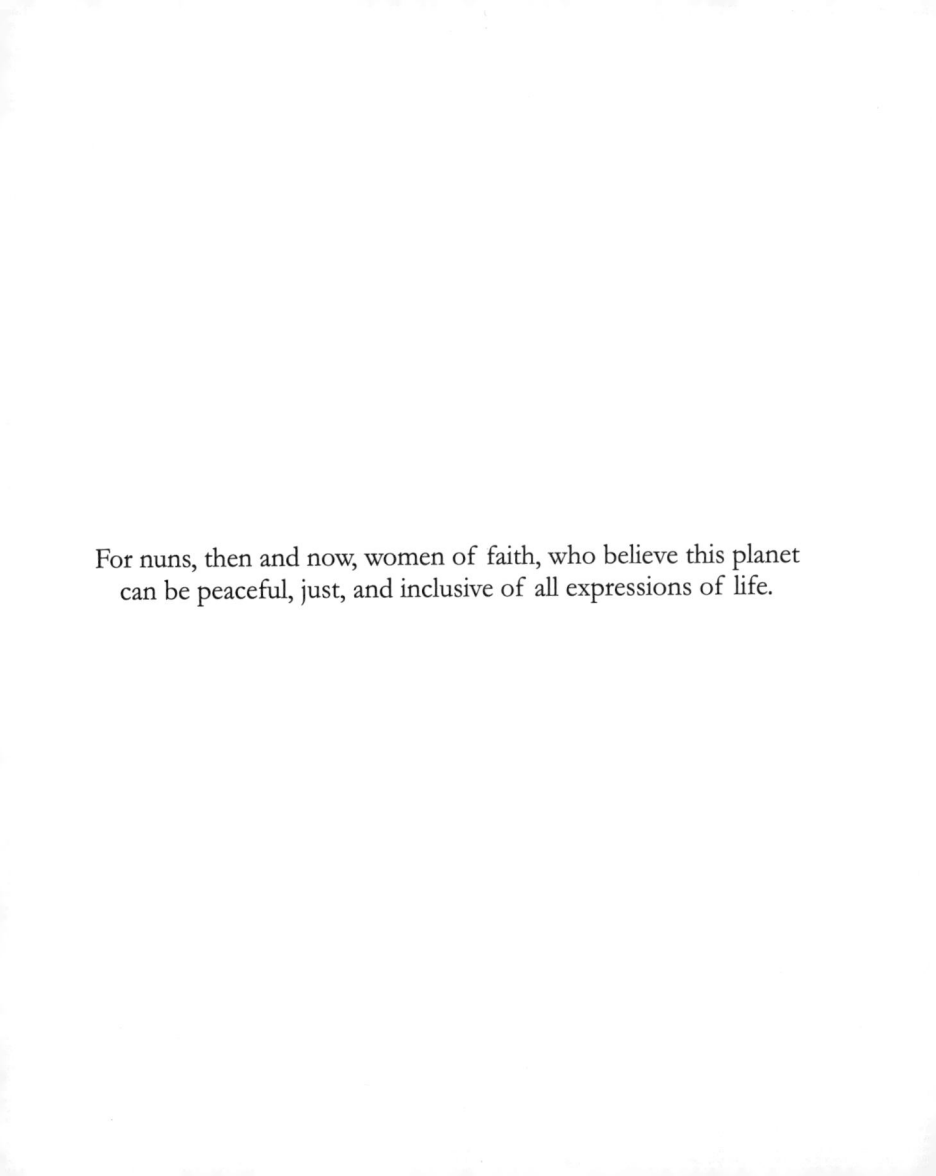

For nuns, then and now, women of faith, who believe this planet can be peaceful, just, and inclusive of all expressions of life.

preface

In the September of 1964, instead of continuing to teach, I went into the convent. I entered the novitiate. I didn't see another classroom for three years.

The day I arrived, I was shown my bed in the dormitory. Folded neatly in the center was the clothing of a nun. This became my mode of dress for the next eight years. What follows here are stories of other nuns from the same time, or before, whose stories are no longer replicated.

I wrote *Brides in Black* partly because of suggestions from readers who enjoyed *The Red Dress*, but mostly because of the compelling stories of women from that era. This was a time of incredible change because of influences such as the second Vatican Council (1962-1964), which was intended to open dialogue between the Roman Catholic Church and the modern world. Perhaps the most significant declaration was that of "freedom of conscience" in the document entitled "Dignitatis Humanae". This meant that an individual has the right to make a decision on moral issues such as birth control, based on an informed conscience.

Another powerful instrument of change was the women's liberation movement in the late sixties and early seventies. Women were encouraged to be educated, independent, and in control of their fertility. Career options such as medicine, law, and engineering became possible for the first time in North American history to women.

Poems in *Brides in Black* are based largely on real events. A few of them represent a situation that existed, but required some poetic license to illustrate. Much of the material was the result of interviews I conducted with women who left convents and women who chose to remain in their religious communities.

As a former nun, I can identify with problems that quickly surface when a woman has no experience with politics in the workplace, money, or dating. Most of us left the convent with very little money to start a new life. One woman who left in 1968 had only two hundred and fifty dollars. This was inadequate and unfair. She had taught elementary school for several years while in the community, and was entitled to much more. With so little money, she endured undue anxiety and hardship. Those who lived in convents for more than ten years felt disconnected from their families and were fearful of becoming a burden.

While in the convent, we were forbidden to be alone in a room with any man, even a close relative. Sexuality and sin were so closely bound in my psyche that guilt dominated any exploration of sexuality. I have vivid memories of my first blind date; it was a disaster. One former nun expressed this in a few words: "Sex was worse than murder." Despite these difficulties, most former nuns achieved some degree of success. Many married, while continuing to teach, nurse, or pursue a university degree. Some embraced a form of ministry, such as Habitat for Humanity.

I found the stories of women who have remained in religious communities to be quite fascinating. Over the past forty years, these communities have witnessed their members dwindle to small groups of older women. Many convents have closed. Young women experienced convents as largely unchanged in terms of medieval attitudes and philosophy. It is indeed unfortunate that the more open-mindedness that was encouraged by Vatican Two was stifled by deeply conservative influences. One very dedicated sister told me that her vow of service to the poor sustains her. She hopes that nuns will have their place in history as founders of hospitals, schools, shelters, and homes for the aged.

A nun who still teaches music is in communication with some of the American nuns who have been secretly ordained as priests. One of them, Patricia Freisen, has been consecrated as a bishop, which gives her the power to ordain other women. Some female priests are married, while others are single or lesbian. Female priests are not limited by a vow of chastity, and are more representative of human experience.

This "underground movement" signals hope for significant change within the church. For the brave women who have been ex-communicated by the Vatican, the road to change has been a difficult one. Rosa Parks and Nelson Mandela challenged unjust laws that upheld racism and intolerance. These individuals serve as a courageous example to contemporary individuals seeking transformation in the church. In a recent university address, Bishop Patricia Freisen affirmed the right of women to become priests no matter what hardships Rome imposes. She quoted Nelson Mandela, "The road is made by walking."

who am i

sinner seductress trickster witch
eve delilah salome jezebel
salacious women
pop out from pages
only on sundays

leader peace maker war hero faithful spouse
esther ruth judith rebekah
a few mumbled verses
only on weekdays
lost in empty cathedrals
as if they might appear
in a sunday sanctuary
clothed in white vestments
threaded with gold
and preach from the pulpit

power of illusion

breasts torso hips vagina legs
evidence of womanhood
hidden beneath robes of religion
sister john paul
sister augustine
sister michael francis
sister st. gregory
high school principals
hospital directors
university department heads
long before betty friedan and gloria steinam
freed women from kitchens nurseries bedrooms
nuns
scented with signs of manhood
scrubbed faces framed in linen
small feet shod in oxfords
entered forbidden worlds
their male names
engraved on glossy office doors

separate menus

succulent salmon
charbroiled steak
roasted vegetables
fresh homemade pies
clear clink of crystal
chilled wines from the cellar
enough loud laughter
to spill over every chalice
on feast days
from the priests' dining room

down the hall
nuns seated at sparse convent tables
saturday night supper
one hardboiled egg
two tablespoons of applesauce
a dry biscuit
lukewarm tea
measured in a small metal pot

two roads

celine is seventeen
accepted to a music school
her talent fills recital halls
bach rachmaninoff debussey
alive in every note every phrase
the audience silent
until celine stands and bows

a priest speaks
god's will is to enter the convent
celine gives away
dresses skirts coats
gold indigo fuchsia
puts on a postulant dress
drab and black
she performs concerts
for grateful nuns
movements of a concerto
harmonies of praise
melodies of prayer
sacred as silence

saturday ceremony

a father watches
his youngest daughter
take vows in a cathedral
cynthia becomes
sister st. boniface
a bride of christ
clothed in the habit
of a twelfth-century abbess
curly hair shorn beneath
a medieval headpiece
flawless face hidden behind
folds of woven cloth
long measure of black

in a soft voice he questions
is my daughter still able
to breathe

from her father's house

at sixteen
beatrice can no longer
breathe in her father's house
fifteen brothers and sisters
sleep in cots
on the living room rug
in musty corners
of the attic

she longs for spaces
to spread pages of learning
to become a woman of words
the convent on the hill
has many rooms
many doors
she doesn't know
there are locks
keys she'll never find

missing daughter

a man whose wife
sleeps in a grave
covered with tears
leaves his only daughter
in the care of nuns
vows to return
on her sixteenth birthday
to take her home

women in black and white
promise the grieving girl
she'll be a bride of god
offer a silky veil
roses embroidered
along every perfect edge

the day before her sixteenth birthday
bernice becomes sister josephine
sister superior tells her father
there's no one named bernice
on these holy grounds

your daughter isn't here

bride of christ

sister esther wonders
who invented
the bride of christ
illusion
the way she covered herself
in white silk
full breasts alive sensuous
until she changed
into plain brown and gray
lovely hair scissored
scattered on the floor
a bride even the saviour
refused to kiss

tonight she stands
before her husband
naked lovely
as any virgin
they kiss deeply
sex is their communion
transformation of ordinary
flesh and blood
ecstasy of saints

instinct

sister philippa
cares for babies
awaiting adoption
superiors warn her
never hold kiss caress a child
maternal instinct lurks
a fire that must be stomped out
smothered
buried
like something dead

on bitter winter nights
when the furnace fails
she carries infants into her narrow cot
pulls a thin blanket tight
curves her body close
to their tiny hearts
for fear
they'll stop

suffer the little children

vivient teaches
in a poor area of town
little children
open their arms
for a hug

her principal a nun
knows vivien also wore
religion on her breast
she takes vivien aside
a teacher must never
show affection
to any child

vow of service

sister jean
believes she's been called
to a life of service
with immigrants the sick
she fills out forms
finds homes for families
schools for girls and boys
who've never learned
to read to write their names
children without
shoes crayons pencils books

doubts about the church
gather like a murder of crows
sister jean keeps silence
trusts in familiar words
i was hungry
and you fed me

she fills another soup bowl
hands it to him

divinity of desire

sister angeline
studies at a college
far from convent walls
wears a summer habit
shine of auburn hair

the chaplain claims
she needs spiritual solace
visits her room
brings red wine
fresh bread and cheese
father philipe takes her hand
caresses each finger
draws her into
the warm circle of his arms
gentle as a groom
with his bride

sister angeline begins
to trust his celibate tongue
consecrated hands
all over her body

silver locket

maureen is thirteen
an orphan in the cloister
a silver locket conceals
the only photo of her parents
michael and rose
they smile
as if they hold her still

at sixteen
she takes final vows
strict nuns command her
to destroy the sacred image
of father
of mother
her only treasure
only link with love

sixty years later
she still weeps
grasps an empty locket
relic of her mother's smile
her father's eyes
faint trace of blood
holy bread of family

seal of confession

sister celine listens
to mia play
rachmaninoff's concerto
in c minor
surprising force of passion
the teacher has never heard
such profound expression
she questions the girl
what's different today
mia admits to an escape
magic of marijuana

sister celine seals mia's confession
tells her to prepare
for tomorrow's concert
practice practice practice
maybe another secret smoke

a virgin for his bed

in sub-saharan africa
father henry fears aids
from prostitutes
he knocks on convent doors
threatens to cut supplies
water corn grain
demands young sister senna
his safeguard against disease
her virginity a red scar
across the face
of the desert moon
her conception
shameful sign of sin
father henry watches
a naked blade enter
senna's swollen body

she bleeds his baby
into sand

road to paradise

sister st. lucien
removes her heavy habit
patched underskirts bloomers buttoned camisole
wriggles into black lace panties
skimpy bra
tight sweater
red miniskirt
she loosens long tresses
all the way down
her slender back
pink lip gloss
hot colour of kisses
becomes lorrie may

at a bar
men gather around
one invites her
for a moon lit ride
mansions of heaven
along the way
maybe an angel counsels her
lorrie may is not dressed for paradise
she leaves alone

jezebel

lorrie may
begins to teach
in a school
run by nuns
from the convent
where she took her vows

the principal strides
spotless halls
rosary clicking
like a bomb
set to blow

she scolds lorrie may
sleeveless tops short skirts
ridiculous heels
if only this cheap jezebel
would cover herself
like a decent catholic girl

it's not right to tempt
the parish priest

diploma

in her seventeenth year
sister francesca vanishes
from silent convent halls
enrols in a catholic high school
to complete her diploma
familiar nuns frown
at scarlet lips
long red hair
short plaid kilt

a tall protestant boy
parks at the front door
every day francesca steps
into his flashy corvette
snuggles close

women in black habits
watch through windows
cross themselves
francesca waves
throws a kiss

convent affairs

the new pastor
presents himself at the convent
a designer tee
sexy summer shorts
soft leather sandals
hints of french cologne

father carl presses the host
firmly into soft smooth hands
sister emma sister louise
he offers spiritual counsel
secrets of sainthood
in papered rectory rooms
warmth of fireplaces
brandy and wine

sister superior stares
into his eyes
tells the priest
to leave young sisters alone

within a week
father carl closes her music school
removes every piano
strips convent tables bare

an apple in her hand

she's the wily serpent from eden
who has crept into his sanctuary
the young woman
who stands before him
offers a round red apple
succulent fruit
plucked from satan's favourite tree

hannah
no longer sister mary blaise
introduces herself to the parish priest
but without her white habit
and the way he stares
eyes scanning the bright bodice
of her flowered dress

she feels naked

silly suits

ella begins university classes
dresses like any student
thrives on campus life

weekends in the convent
she must hide herself
with a silly suit
blue skirt shapeless navy jacket
hair tightly pulled back
under a thick veil

her history professor visits
wonders who she is
his student transformed
into a postulant of the past

caught in tangled threads
of faith

letters of lent

letters from home
are withheld
advent and lent
eleven weeks of each year
without a word

names scribbled
envelopes torn
messages stale as ash
left on a numbered shelf
above the superior's desk
parents brothers sisters
connections broken and blurred

ella and her family
must follow
rules of a nunnery

empty house

ella watches new members
of her community
leave every week
some have been
in the convent
less than a year
others disappear
after a few september days
their absence a wound
swollen festered red

where can you go
what can you build

the house is empty

ex-con

ella asks to open a bank account
applies for a charge card

the manager searches for credit history
nothing appears
he frowns
asks where she's lived
for the past twenty years
she explains about the convent
her vow of poverty

the bank declines
ella feels like a woman
who's been convicted
forced to wear an anklet
that tracks every move

baggage

sister sarah ann
keeps losing weight
her superiors suspect pride
delusions of sainthood
a failure who must leave

on the late night train
she stares into a mirror
blotchy face already creased
brown hair scissored to the scalp
cheap wrinkled suit
three sizes too large

she is an orphan
an outcast with a suitcase

in a red sweater

rick frequents the diner
buck teeth
greasy brown hair
a black thunderbird
he invites sarah ann
the new waitress
for burgers
movies at the drive-in
snaps a photo
sarah ann convent reject
in a red sweater
blown up
for his bedroom wall

they're engaged
rick begins to follow her
watches at night from across the street
phones whenever friends come to visit
sarah ann believes he cares
wants to keep her safe

secret of virginity

she dates a soldier
returned from vietnam
a man who's stepped over death
in fields rotted with blood
counted broken skulls
piled body bags into trucks
numbers without names

he needs to suckle
a woman's breasts
taste the first kiss of her tongue
open sweet secrets of virginity

sarah ann fears
the sear of sin
all over her soul
he walks away
from her vietnam
embraces a woman
who holds him
through a whole night of peace

marriage to a thief

a man she believes
loves and cares for her
marries sarah ann

in their first year
he becomes distant
absent from their bed
sarah ann blames herself
tries to be a better wife

on their anniversary
he is arrested for fraud
takes an overdose
survives
she forgives him
makes love every night

within a month
sarah ann is pregnant
chained to a thief

survival skills

after twelve years
gwen leaves a convent
clutching a cheque
eighteen hundred dollars
she's never shopped
never worn lipstick
never had a date
a teller shows her
how to open an account
how to write a cheque
gwen thinks she's rich

in a dealership
gwen announces
she'd like a yellow car
the salesman smiles
asks what model
what year
her price range
if she'd like to drive
the corvette on the lot
gwen excuses herself
says she will wait

at university
gwen attends science class
returns to her room
she's heard students joke
about the pub
gwen's never been in a pub
never ordered food
or a drink

in physics lab
a tall slender blonde
who drives a red ferrari
meets with gwen
shows her everything
how to bargain for a car
how to work
the student pub
bare legs
high heels
bright lip gloss
tight tops
before gwen knew only
how to study
how to pray
now she has answers
forbidden by convent rules
freedoms she can't wait
to explore to embrace

makeover

nell gets off the bus
pale skin tied back hair
shapeless brown dress
cut from convent cloth

her sister takes nell
to an upscale salon
long layers
blonde highlights
a makeup artist
applies bronze blush mascara lip gloss
pink polish on fingers and toes

nell wants to slip
into a little black dress
high heels
shiny and red
she smiles
at the pretty woman
in bevelled glass
a stranger

virgin in a bar

a man in a bar
can smell a convent virgin
her hesitation
in the slow
curl of smoke
incense of nicotine

as she pushes against the varnished door
luke smiles
offerings of tequila and rye
a new saviour
who leans close
keys to a kingdom
only he can reveal

vivien takes his hand
believes every word
chapter and verse

boarding house

in her first stormy summer
loneliness falls upon amanda
like black rain

she moves into a boarding house
damp room with a small window
dreary as any convent cell
every week new faces
wary eyes cast down

no one from the nunnery
calls to ask if she's safe
if she needs anything
as if they've erased
ten precious years
ripped up her breviary
matins lauds vespers
evening song of compline
tossed every word
into fiery furnaces
of their fabled hell

you have a job

alma receives one thousand dollars
from the convent
she needs cash for rent food clothes
a car
her family is distant
too many years of letters
now and then
too many visits in a crowded
sunday space

alma becomes frightened
moves into a first floor flat
mouldy walls shabby rugs
bicycle on the balcony
she pleads with the nuns
for more money
mother superior
pounds her fist
on a tidy desk
tells alma she has a job
she'll have to find her way

she waits for a bus
in the january dawn

another failure

gwen and tom
step away from
safe sanctuaries
convent and monastery
return to ordinary pews
jobs in the city
subways buses

they delay a diamond
cancel a wedding hall
fearful of another failure

gwen decides
she's moving in
they learn the daily dance
a one room space
a single bed
how love transcends
fear of failure

sisters on campus

gail meets young nuns
from her community
friends only a month ago
they shun her
she's the child of judas
who'll bribe each of them
into betrayal
have them change
into scandalous shorts
strappy sandals
sexy as sin

gail sits alone
far from sisters of faith
pretending they've never
shared supper
at long covered tables
never chanted prayers
in chapel stalls
close enough to touch

dollars and sense

for twenty years
edna knelt to ask
permission for underwear
permission for shoes
permission for an aspirin

now on her own
money is a mystery
rent hydro food
as if she can walk
into an apartment
light a candle
whisper a prayer
watch rooms fill with furniture
closets overflow with clothes

a friend signs for a loan
warns edna
to measure out every dollar
as if she's still in a convent
still needs permission to exist

parish social

a soldier on leave
asks giselle to dance
all you need is love
somewhere in the song
slow caress of hands
he moves
too close for chastity

for a whole year
she slowly stripped away
yards of convent garb
shiny linens
scratch of starch
against her skin

now his mouth is on hers
tongue inside

perimeters

months after the last convent meal
three meet for dinner
worries gather like crows
on a wet wire
money jobs clothes rent
a man at the far table
sends over a bottle of champagne
he's in the city on business
hates his lonely room

nothing said of silent convent cells
scratchy blankets iron cots
breath of icy windows
lips blue as death
let him think they've mastered this dance
that they know every step
brings them closer
to a cliff
perimeters they pretend not to see
every turn perilous

first and last month's rent

sister mary gertrude
has answered convent bells
since she was twelve
she knows nothing
of money and men
pays first and last month's rent
buys a table bed chair

the manager uses his key
steals her mother's ring
sneaks into the bedroom
takes lacy panties and bras
calls after midnight
leaves filthy messages
after mary confronts him
she finds car windows smashed
mouldings sliced

a detective warns
she'll be next

first date

for nine winters
nell slept
in a cold convent bed
restless dreams of an open door
moonlight down the steps

her first date
is arranged by friends
she and paul meet
in a dingy diner
he shakes nell's hand
forces a smile
studies her face
as if she has wrinkles and warts

the burger and fries
go cold
on nell's plastic plate
her friends were mistaken
paul is much younger
maybe seven years
maybe more
he stares out the window
nell conceals herself
in silence
a familiar veil

loss of innocence

gwen visits her brother
space of twelve convent years
a gap they try to fill
one gin and tonic
after another
laughter jokes

they switch
to bitter lemon

gwen is heaving
over the toilet
certain of death
a poisoning
jim stands at the door
laughing
he tells his sister
this is a hangover

strangers at the table

after twenty years
sister st. matthew
returns home
as helen sims

the house she left
seems smaller
as if winds
pressed against walls
snow and ice
flattened the roof
soaked through memories
of childhood
parents and siblings
strangers at the table
communion of silence
helen's smile missing
from photos held in wooden frames
marriages birthdays baptisms

migrants

sister margarite
signs papers to annul her vows
in a cloister
where nothing is wanting
clean beds meals on the table
sheltered nights and days

she marries a man
who trusts her ways
together they assist migrants
sweaty men who move farm to farm
teach them english
give them bicycles
warm sweaters in the fall

her convent vows transformed
in the circle of her table
in the celebration of sunday fiestas
food prepared for others
hands joined with brothers of christ
thin bodies skin blistered
from twelve hours in the sun
wives and children
along borders of mexico
waiting to be fed

forbidden art

superiors lock
the pandora's box
of her art
keep sister virginia away
from water colours pastels
flagrant oils
scarlet purple indigo

when she ends convent life
an art school
embraces her gift
celebrates passion
beautiful bodies
all the hidden forbidden
delicious delights
breasts lips tongues

slow tango

celine embraces music
she plays
variations of the slow tango
by astor piazzolla invierno portena
perfect pitch of sound

celine fears sensual steps
mortal sin all over the floor
her body moves into the dance
long black skirt silk crimson blouse
glimmers of shame
redeemed in mirrors
along the shadowed wall
beauty pure as any sacrament
white flame of a candle
burning through the night

rhythms

sister st. monica
leaves the convent in a checkered cab
begins to teach piano and voice
earns just enough to rent a room
buy some clothes and shoes
the father of one of her students
lingers every week
a widower who also sleeps alone
he offers marriage
a house with a piano
his only love song
notes she's never heard
rhythms she's never played

under pain of sin

sister fiona scorns convent rules
returns to ireland
a small cottage by the sea
pets sleepy dogs
she kindles her fire
writes popular novels
mystery love sex

the parish priest
preaches against her
no one must read
a single page
of fiona's filth
under pain of grievous sin

a fallen woman
who keeps company
with a divorced man
her cottage a nest of vipers
her bed a breeding place
for satan's seed

medical doctor

sister laura
a brilliant nurse
asks to study
for a medical degree
superiors frown
suspicions of arrogance
she's told to leave the convent
no place for young nuns
who wish to go beyond
the holy will of god
laura walks down marble stairs
one small satchel in her hand

doctor laura
treats old nuns with failing hearts
they never guess
the tall young woman who eases their pain
wore the same veil
kept the same rules

sealed shut

years after nell's vows
dissolve in vatican vaults
she dreams a return to long convent halls
still slippery from pasty wax
she rubbed on endless floors

there are no windows
every door is locked
dusty lights flicker
shadowy nuns kneel in corners

nell clutches papers from rome
signed by the bishop
permission to leave
she begins to race
through the marble chapel
to an exit in the vestry
she finds it sealed shut
smooth mortar still fresh
as if god
won't let her go

cold chapel

pearl lives alone
fingers swollen and sore
palms creased with age
her fortune
has never been told
priceless youth sealed
in a cold chapel
where winter crept
into the stain of glass
stole shades of loveliness
shining glimmers of light

too many years
in a convent
keep pearl
in a small room
narrow window streaked
with shades of gray

when i was sick

sister marie thomas
removes her cross
in a winter of doubt
works in a downtown shop
stumbles into marriage

illness traps
an aging woman
unheated house broken pipes
meals of toast and tea
unwashed body unwashed hair

marie's husband leaves

she asks to return
to the care of nuns
they welcome her
as if she'd never gone
as if they are sisters
of blood

noises in the night

sister joan folds her habit
into a convent box
rents a ninth floor flat
clamours in the night
footsteps on the fire escape
police at her door
a gifted pianist
destined for carnegie hall
murdered in her bed
just two floors below

joan stands nine floors above chaos
recalls sounds sifted from sleep
feels the discord of her days
strident tones of nights
peaceful chimes of vespers lost

she whispers into darkness
it should have been me

convent inheritance

after the funeral mass
of linda's aunt
a nun takes her aside
hands her a shoe box
brown umbrella
black rosary beads
four white-tipped pins
one blank sheet
paper folded in half
faded fountain pen

linda stares at steel pins
that held together
scratchy bands of linen
worn for sixty years
she touches paper and pen
ponders what sister mary leo
wanted to write
silence she needed to break

legacy

the convent on the corner
freezes in rain
shutters swing
in november winds
wild ivy tangles
across icy walls
of kitchen refectory
novitiate dormitory chapel
asleep in the day
empty even of god
tabernacle left open
in case he returns

the bus once filled
with voices of nuns
on their way to hospitals
soup-kitchens shelters schools
rests on wooden blocks
far from turns
of the gravel road

silence without sun
bears the weight
of prayer worry work
compassion
preserved from decay

novices

forty years ago
white veils
filled front pews
of the convent chapel
as if young angels chose to appear
before the high alter

novices called to be nuns
vanish through windows
painted for the sun
nameless prayer books shut
hymns of praise
lost in pages
numbered in dust

now sisters shuffle
with walkers
strain to hear the priest

convent for sale

fifty elderly nuns board the last bus
from their convent of four hundred rooms
esther assists with the move
their journey leads
to a nursing home
a tent in the desert
uncertain temporary
foreign to old women
ester feels the stare
of failing eyes
questions escape
through tinted glass
did i waste my life
should i have left
how do i breathe
in tatters of a remnant
patterns faded frayed
left too long in the dark

how could this happen
to brides of christ

side door

ten years after
her last convent meal
nell still goes to mass
the priest in his high pulpit
she in a crowded pew
his sermon
words from the vatican

nell will never see
a woman
vested in the sanctuary
prophetic vision
messenger of change

the side door closes
god is only a shadow
on the steps

nell leaves him there

anonymous

sister simone
returns from five years
in bolivia
weary from long days
nights in the clinic

she reads an article
in the morning paper
praise for the mission
of the diocese in bolivia
a photo of every priest
names loud as sermons
from a bishop's pulpit

nuns appear in small print
black and white phantoms
from a local convent
no photos no names
to honour their parents
sacrifice of daughters

hidden

in a cathedral
sisters sweep dust polish shine
every inch of the sanctuary
trim white summer blooms
others unfurl linen cloths
starched and pressed
one lights a tall candle
blinks in the flame

a small bell sounds
every nun vanishes
before the grand procession
a bishop's consecration

nuns disappear into blossoms
no names inscribed in gold
absent from glory

convocation

a brilliant nun
studies theology
places first in her class
the chancellor
sends for her

she has permission
to take every course
write a thesis
even a consecrated virgin
who conceals her body
in deepest black
will never be called
to convocation
never hold a theology degree
with her name
sister grace brennan
illumined in hallowed halls
burnished doors open
only to men

witch in the seminary

in an ivy-covered seminary
sister grace teaches
freedom of conscience
informed decisions
birth control divorce re-marriage
she decries
brutal oppression of women
cruel bondage of sex

sister grace knows
seminarians crave
a mother-figure
to kiss every bruise
she continues to advance
new dimensions of thought
quotes a theologian
dares to question

within a week
the new rector
fires the only woman
ever to speak
in this hallowed space
his eyes glare
reflections from a fire
set for a witch

high horses of rome

after eight years
in slums of bolivia
sister imelda attends mass
in her home parish
hears a sermon on priests
true emissaries of christ
heroes of the church
blessed at the last supper

sister imelda pens a letter

priests are only part of the church
it's time priests
were struck down
from high horses of rome
women are also baptized
into the kingdom
yet banned from altars
where christ still waits
to welcome them

sacred scent

sister elizabeth
is ordained in secret
the bishop places his hands
on her head
shapes the sign of the cross
with holy oil
then he kneels
asks for her blessing

for seven days
elizabeth can smell
the fragrance of chrism
sacred scent of priesthood
held in her hair
she reflects on st. clare
an ancient cathedral
sacrifice of her golden hair
scissors in the hands
of a humble monk
francis of assisi

consecration in munich

sister catherine stands
before a bishop in munich
a few candles
illumine the altar
twelve nuns and priests
witness him place his hands
on catherine's head
intone sacred words
consecration of a woman
as bishop
power to ordain other women
in persona christi

catherine feels on her hair
the fall of tears
the bishop weeps
as jesus did
when he called lazarus
into the dawn

the new priesthood

bishop catherine knows
she'll never have a diocese
live in a mansion by the sea
ride in a chauffeured car
flash a rubied ring

she wears a silk stole
her small wooden cross
crafted by a carpenter
offers mass in a basement
invites other women
to partake of the priesthood
bread and wine
of the new covenant
free of vows to celibacy
open to marriage

catherine anoints each woman
sacred blessing of a sacrament
power of holy orders
her hands consecrated with grace

she is a bishop
with breasts

renewal

women answer the call
climb the hill
return to empty halls
airless rooms
mingle with sisters
then and now
flashbacks of anger
swept out
into the river
lifted with laughter
bonds shaped in another life

a breath of redemption
received with thanks
before heavy oak doors
lock every crucifix inside

acknowledgements

Brides in Black began as a suggestion from Marty Gervais to write a collection of poems based on experiences of women who left and women who chose to stay in convents. What started out as simply an idea rapidly became a project of great interest.

In the process of writing this book, I interviewed several women who left convents in North America over the last forty years. I also interviewed women who chose to remain in their communities. These women provided fascinating stories and experiences on which this collection is based. I'm deeply grateful to all of the women who spoke with me. Penny-Anne Beaudoin provided several contacts for which I am extremely appreciative.

I want to thank the editorial team at Black Moss for the many hours spent meeting, discussing, and designing *Brides in Black*. Their editing suggestions were creative and insightful. I greatly appreciate their talent and dedication. Thank you to Emily Abbott, Emily Buta, Sarah Benoit, Jessica Clemençon, Joshua Dagenais, Sarah Formagin, Victoria Galea, Ashley Gibb, Celia Girgenti, Beth Harrett, Nicole Pelaccia, Jared Pollen, Amelia Roy-Weber, Amanda Spence, Rebecca Taylor, Sarah Wasyluk, Jaclyn Wood and Jordan Turner.

Kate Hargreaves provided creative and informed direction in the design and editing of this book. Marty Gervais provided the guidance and expertise of a publisher, poet, professor, and mentor. I'm deeply grateful to Marty for believing in this project and for staying close to the process.

My family and friends have shown support and interest, and I found this extremely helpful.

table of contents

who am i - 9
power of illusion - 10
separate menus - 11
two roads - 12
saturday ceremony - 13
from her father's house - 14
missing daughter - 15
bride of christ - 16
instinct - 17
suffer the little children - 18
vow of service - 19
divinity of desire - 20
silver locket - 21
seal of confession - 22
a virgin for his bed - 23
road to paradise - 24
jezebel - 25
diploma - 26
convent affairs - 27
an apple in her hand - 28
silly suits - 29
letters of lent - 30
empty house - 31
ex-con - 32
baggage - 33

in a red sweater - 34
secret of virginity - 35
marriage to a thief - 36
survival skills - 37-40
makeover - 41
virgin in a bar - 42
boarding house - 43
you have a job - 44
another failure - 45
sisters on campus - 46
dollars and sense - 47
parish social - 48
perimeters - 49
first and last month's rent - 50
first date - 51
loss of innocence - 52
strangers at the table - 53
migrants - 54
forbidden art - 55
slow tango - 56
rhythms - 57
under pain of sin - 58
medical doctor - 59
sealed shut - 60
cold chapel - 61

when i was sick - 62
noises in the night - 63
convent inheritance - 64
legacy - 65
novices - 66
convent for sale - 67
side door - 68
anonymous - 69
hidden - 70
convocation - 71
witch in the seminary - 72
high horses of rome - 73
sacred scent - 74
consecration in munich - 75
the new priesthood - 76
renewal - 77

acknowledgements - 78